MW00489942

Manuscript

THE
Rhythm
OF HANDWRITING

DENISE EIDE

The Rhythm of Handwriting Manuscript Student Book

Copyright © 2013 Logic of English, Inc
All rights reserved.

No part of this publication may be reproduced, stored in a retrieval system, or transmitted, in any form, or by any means, electronic, mechanical, photocopying, recording, or otherwise without the prior consent of the publisher.

According to the United States Copyright Office, "Copyright infringement occurs when a copyrighted work is reproduced, distributed, performed, publicly displayed, or made into a derivative work without the permission of the copyright owner." For further information, see http://www.copyright.gov/help/faq/faq-definitions.html.

Logic of English® is a Registered Trademark of Logic of English, Inc.
Printed in the United States of America.

Logic of English, Inc
4865 19th Street NW, Suite 130
Rochester, MN 55901

Cover Design: Dugan Design Group
Interior design and typesetting: Katherine Lloyd, The Desk
LOE School Font: David Occhino Design

ISBN 978-1-936706-26-6

First Edition

10 9 8 7 6 5 4 3

www.LogicOfEnglish.com

TABLE OF CONTENTS

STEPS TO
TEACHING HANDWRITING

The twenty-six letters of the alphabet are the basis for writing the 75 basic phonograms which describe 98% of English words. For students who are new to the Logic of English® it is best to combine teaching the sounds of the single-letter phonograms with learning how to write them.

The *Rhythm of Handwriting* series provides both explicit instruction and rhythmic language which aids the development of muscle memory. Research has shown that students who write fluently and legibly have a clear understanding of how each letter is formed, rhythmic handwriting which pauses only at the natural stopping points, and automatic muscle memory so they are not struggling to remember how to form each letter.

In order to facilitate mastery, letters are organized by their initial strokes. In this way students will have concentrated practice developing the muscle memory needed for these letters.

Before beginning to teach how to write the letters, introduce the lines on the Handwriting Chart on page 17, or use the *Logic of English Whiteboard.* Show the students the baseline, top line, and midline. Then ask them to repeat back the name of each line.

Teachers may choose whether or not to teach the strokes needed to form each letter. Some students benefit from isolated stroke instruction, whereas others gain more by seeing how all the pieces fit together. The strokes needed for each letter are listed at the beginning of each section.

1. Show the students the Basic Phonogram Flash Card of the targeted letter. (These may be purchased at www.LogicOfEnglish.com/store.)

2. Say the sound(s) found on the back of the flashcard.

3. Ask the students to repeat the sound(s). (Correct errors in pronunciation.)

4. Using the workbook, show the students how the phonogram appears in handwriting. Discuss how the handwritten form is the same as the bookface form and how it is different.

5. Using the Handwriting Chart, point to where the letter begins and identify it aloud. Demonstrate with your pointer finger how to write the first step of the letter while saying the directions aloud.

6. Ask the students to point to where the letter begins, identify its location, and demonstrate the first step of the letter and repeat the directions aloud.

7. Demonstrate the first and second steps while saying the directions aloud.

8. Ask the students to repeat the first and second steps while saying the directions. (Continue in this manner until all the steps have been introduced.)

9. Ask the students to repeat forming the letter while saying the directions aloud 2-3 times. End by saying the sound(s) made by the letter.

10. Model the letter using the shortened bold instructions. Emphasize the rhythm. End by saying the sound(s) made by the letter.

11. Ask the students to model correct formation 3-5 times while stating the rhythmic directions, followed by the letter's sound(s). Check to make sure that the students are developing fluid and rhythmic motions.

12. Optional: Direct the students to trace the enlarged letter in the workbook with their pointer fingers or practice with the Rhythm of Handwriting Tactile Cards. Check that the students are demonstrating fluid, rhythmic motions.

STUDENTS WITH UNDEVELOPED FINE-MOTOR SKILLS

13. Practice the letter using large-motor motions on the *Logic of English Whiteboard*, a chalkboard, or in a sensory box. Practice fine-motor skills by using scissors, coloring, and other activities. When the students' motor skills have developed, move on to step 14.

STUDENTS WITH DEVELOPED FINE-MOTOR SKILLS

14. Practice writing the letter on paper with a pencil. Allow students to choose the line size that is most comfortable and results in the most legible writing.

Handwriting Tips

TEACH LOWERCASE LETTERS FIRST

Lowercase letters comprise more than 90% of all that we read and write. Uppercase letters are only used at the beginning of sentences and with proper nouns. Teaching lowercase letters first provides students with the most vital information they need to be successful in learning to read and write.

Once students have mastered the lowercase letters, they should be taught how to write the capital letters and how to use them properly.

TEACH HANDWRITING USING ALL FOUR LEARNING MODES

When teaching students how to write, always use all four learning modalities: seeing, hearing, doing, and speaking. Show the students how to form the letter (seeing) while providing explicit spoken directions (hearing). Then ask the students to repeat the action (doing) while repeating the directions aloud (speaking).

TEACH EACH LETTER WITH LARGE-MOTOR MOVEMENTS

Teach letter formation using large muscle movements originating from the elbow. Demonstrate the motions using your pointer finger on the enlarged handwriting charts provided in the book. Students should then imitate the motions using their pointer fingers and movements that originate from the elbow. Once the motions have been learned, students should practice the sequence of movements on the *Logic of English Whiteboard*, on a chalkboard, in the air, or in sensory boxes.

The *Logic of English Whiteboards* can be valuable at this stage as students can practice letter formation holding a marker but using large-motor movements that originate from the elbow rather than fine-motor movements that originate in the fingers. Textured letters such as sandpaper letters are also useful as they engage the student's large-motor memory with a high sensory experience.

PROVIDE CLEAR AND EXPLICIT DIRECTIONS
ON HOW TO FORM EACH LETTER

Some students who have poor handwriting are unclear about how to form the letters and how they relate to the lines on the page. When teaching, it is important to provide students with full, explicit directions on letter formation, leaving no room for confusion. Each letter in the *Rhythm of Handwriting* series includes explicit directions for introducing the letters. Students who are sensitive to too much auditory input may learn each letter using only the rhythmic, bold instructions as described below.

EMPHASIZE THE RHYTHM OF HANDWRITING

Fluent handwriting is rhythmic with pauses only at the natural stopping or reversal points in the letters. Other than the natural stopping points, the pencil should continue in a steady motion. The bold keywords in the *Rhythm of Handwriting* materials provide students with abbreviated directions which accent the natural rhythm of each letter.

STROKES OR NO STROKES?

Some students benefit greatly by learning the strokes in isolation before learning how to write each letter. These students usually see each letter as a puzzle that is formed by putting the pieces of the strokes together. Other students feel confused by learning the strokes in isolation and have the greatest success by learning how to write each letter as a whole. Experiment to find your student's learning style by teaching a few strokes on pages 16-17. Practice writing the strokes with the pointer finger on the handwriting chart provided. Continue to practice the strokes on the *Logic of English Whiteboard*. If the student finds this helpful, continue in the same manner with the following chapters. If the student was confused by learning the strokes individually, then skip the strokes pages in later chapters and move straight into teaching the letters.

PROVIDE SUPPORT

Until students have mastered how to form the letters with ease, they should not be left alone to practice. When beginner students see a letter, they automatically tend to focus on copying a visual image. This detracts from building the muscle memory needed to write fluidly. In addition, for some students the visual image is easy to reverse in their minds, making it more likely for them to struggle with reversals in both handwriting and reading. Clear, explicit teaching using all the learning modalities will eliminate confusion about letter directions.

Careful guidance from the beginning will prevent bad habits from forming. If teachers invest time to ensure that each student develops correct muscle memory for each letter and understands how each is formed, huge amounts of wasted time and pain will be avoided in the future for both writing and reading.

Students should not be asked to copy words, sentences, or paragraphs until they are able to read the words and sentences they are copying. When asked to do so sooner, the task is akin to art and is void of any language learning value. Copywork is valuable once students are making speech-to-print connections. In order to recognize the connection between speech and print, students should first practice writing letters and phonograms from dictation. The teacher should say the sound(s) made by the letter and the students should write the letter on a whiteboard, on paper, or in a sensory box. Once students have mastered several of the single-letter phonograms and are able to write them fluidly, they may begin to combine the single-letter phonograms into words. Ideally words will also be taught through dictation. When students begin to practice their handwriting through copywork as found in the *Rhythm of Handwriting* series, they should read the word aloud, then practice writing it while sounding it out aloud.

CROSSING T'S AND F'S

Students should cross the lowercase "t" and "f" in the direction of reading and writing, i.e. from left to right. The uppercase letters A, E, F, H, I, and T should also be crossed in the direction of reading and writing.

TRANSITIONING TO PENCIL AND PAPER

The decision to transition to pencil and paper should be based upon the age, development, and prior experiences of the student. Many older students will find great success in learning to write a letter using large-motor skill with the handwriting chart, then immediately writing the letter with a pencil.

Students with less developed fine-motor skills benefit from extended large-motor practice. By learning letter formation with movements that originate from the elbow as opposed to the fingers, students are programming the motions and rhythms into their brains. The muscle memory which is formed using large-motor movements will translate into fine-motor motions.

Once the students have mastered forming a letter using large-motor motions with their pointer fingers, they may transition to writing the letters on a whiteboard, chalkboard, sensory box or other texture writing. This practice will help to cement the motions and the letter shapes in their minds. If a student is lagging with fine-motor development, writing exercises may be done in large-motor movements using a whiteboard or chalkboard until his fine-motor development is sufficient for writing.

During this time students should also be engaged in fine-motor activities on a daily basis. Many of the examples below require adult supervision.

- Color with markers, chalk, crayons, and other media.
- Provide the students with an eyedropper and small paper cups. Fill one cup with water. Direct students to transfer the water with the eyedropper. For added fun, use a few drops of food coloring in each cup and allow students to experiment with mixing colors.
- Make necklaces and bracelets with plastic beads.
- Use tweezers to move beads from one cup to another.
- Provide students with small colored pom-poms and direct them to sort them by color.
- Provide clothespins that pinch. String a rope between two chairs and allow students to hang up doll clothes, socks, or pictures to display.
- Use child-safe scissors.
- Provide students with bolts, nuts, and washers of varying sizes to sort and screw together.
- Play with building toys.

Many students will benefit from some or all of the following tips when transitioning from large-motor movements to writing on paper. Clear and explicit teaching can prevent unnecessary confusion and provide students with the support they need to succeed.

PENCIL GRIP

Instruct the students how to hold the pencil with the thumb and the first finger so the pencil rests gently on the middle finger. If the student struggles to hold the pencil correctly, provide a pencil grip.

PAPER POSITION

Demonstrate how to place the paper at an angle so the arm naturally sweeps from the elbow rather than needing to tense the shoulder or twist the wrist. Ask the students to make curved sweeping lines along the paper, using motions from their elbow. Then position the paper so the student's strokes follow the lines of the paper.

LINE SIZE

This book provides a variety of line sizes for each exercise. Allow the student to experiment. Discuss: which line is the most comfortable? On which size does the student write the most neatly? Which line size is a better fit for the student's hand? In future exercises allow the student to choose the line size that is most comfortable and results in the most legible writing.

Despite conventional wisdom that young students should use paper with giant spaces between the lines, many beginning writers benefit from much smaller lines. Because they have small hands, smaller lines encourage students to use fine-motor movements originating in the fingers without stretching uncomfortably.

Direct the students to practice writing letters on the lines. Encourage them to use motions from the fingers, not the wrist or elbow, to form each letter.

ENCOURAGING MASTERY

It is only through abundant practice that students learn to write fluently. Require daily handwriting practice until all the letters have been mastered. At the end of a practice session, ask the students to evaluate their own writing by picking the letter or word on the page that is written the most neatly and explain why they believe it is the best. Then, as the teacher, choose the letter that you think is written the most neatly and explain why.

For some students the letter may need to be retaught a second or even third day before all motions are mastered. This is particularly true after a weekend or break. Simply repeat the steps, providing clear, explicit instruction. Require students to model the motions correctly while repeating the directions aloud.

SUGGESTED SCHEDULES

STUDENTS AGES SIX AND UNDER

Students six and under should learn one letter per day. Each lesson should include:

- Introduction to a new letter including its sound(s) and how to write it.
- Practice matching sounds to previously learned letters.
- Practice reading previously learned letters.
- Practice writing previously learned letters.

Handwriting games like the ones found on pages 9-10 may be used to enhance review.

Once students have learned how to write a-z and have memorized their sounds, they are ready to begin combining a-z into short words and to begin learning the multi-letter phonograms.

STUDENTS AGES 7 AND UP

Older students who are not familiar with the sounds and/or manuscript forms of A-Z may use one of the following schedules:

SCHEDULE 1

Learn two letters per day starting with the lowercase letters.

SCHEDULE 2

Learn four letters per day starting with the lowercase letters.

SCHEDULE 3

Learn all the letters based upon one initial stroke each day (straight letters, etc.).

IDEAS FOR
HANDWRITING PRACTICE

LETTER DICTATION

Provide students with a whiteboard, chalkboard, sensory box, or paper. Say the sound(s) of one of the letters. Direct the students to write the letter.

BLIND WRITING

Direct the students to close their eyes and write the letter five to ten times without looking. Without visual cues, the students must rely on muscle memory. Instruct the students to open their eyes and choose the letter which is written the most legibly.

SPEED WRITING

Set a timer for 20 seconds. Direct students to write the letter as many times as possible before the timer beeps. Instruct the students to choose the letter that is written most legibly.

TREASURE HUNT

Write the letters that students know on index cards with glitter glue. Hide the letters around the room. Direct students to find the letters and bring them back to you. When they find a letter they must read the sound(s) and demonstrate how to write it on a whiteboard or chalkboard or using the glitter card.

LETTER STATIONS

Set up stations of whiteboards, chalkboards, or sensory boxes around the room. Students will rotate between the stations. Call out the sound(s) of a letter. The students must write the letter at their station. Every two to three letters, rotate to the next station.

SKY WRITING

Call out the sound(s) of a letter. Direct students to write it in the air using their arm and pointer finger.

SIMON SAYS

Appoint one student to be "Simon." Provide the student with a set of flashcards containing all the letters that have been learned. "Simon" draws a card and reads the sound(s). The other students must write the letter on a small whiteboard.

FOOT WRITING

Direct students to lay on their backs on the floor. Call out the sound(s) made by one of the letters. Direct students to write the letter in the air using their foot.

WRITING GAME

Direct two students to sit back to back. Each person will need a small whiteboard. The first person writes a letter on the whiteboard, then tells the other person the directions for writing the letter. The other person then writes the letter. If both people have written the same letter they get one point.

Lowercase Letters

Handwriting Chart

We will be using a handwriting chart like this one to learn how to form each letter. Show the student the baseline, midline, and top line. Ask the student to identify each line and point to it. Direct the student, "Draw a line with your pointer finger from the baseline to the top line." "Draw a line from the midline to the baseline." "Draw a circle that sits between the midline and the top line." "Draw a circle that sits between the midline and the baseline."

STRAIGHT LETTERS

i   t   r

l   b   p

k   h

n   m

STROKES

STRAIGHT

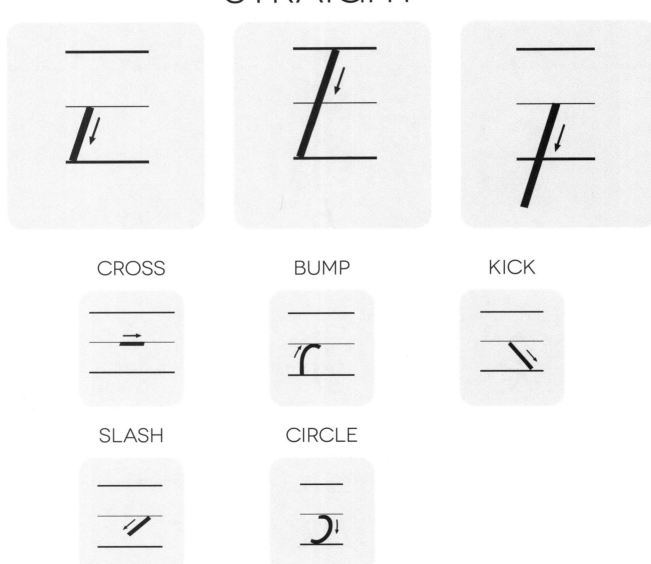

CROSS   BUMP   KICK

SLASH   CIRCLE

Start at the midline. ①**Straight** to the baseline, ②pick up the pencil, ③**dot**.   /ĭ-ī-ē-y/

Start halfway between the top line and the midline. ①**Straight** to the baseline, ②pick up the pencil, ③**cross** at the midline.   /t/

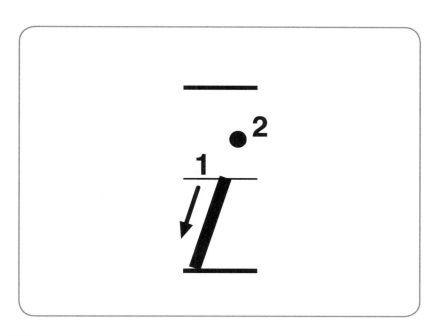

i

i

i

i

i

i

i

i

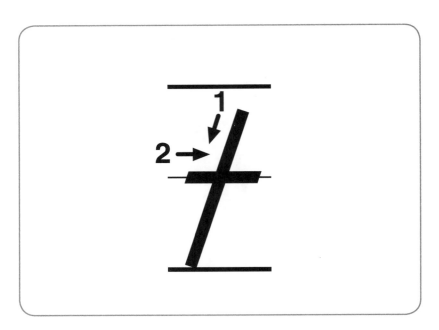

r   *Start at the midline.* ①**Straight** to the baseline, ②**bump** up to the midline.   /r/

l   *Start at the top line.* ①**Straight** to the baseline.   /l/

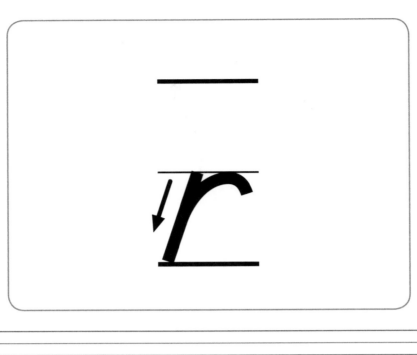

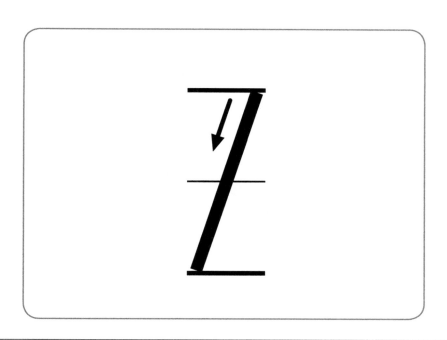

Start at the top line. ①**Straight** to the baseline, ②slide **up** to the midline, ③**circle** around to the baseline, ④touch.   /b/

Start at the midline. ①**Straight** down halfway below the baseline, ②slide **up** to the midline, ③**circle** around to the baseline, ④touch.   /p/

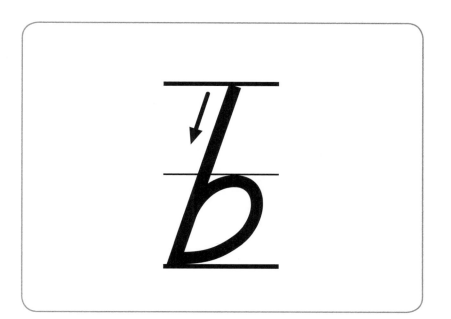

b

b

b

b

b

b

b

b

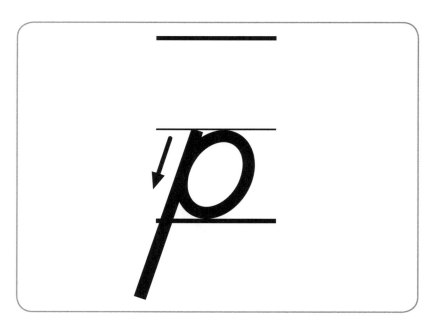

p

p

p

p

p

p

p

p

Start at the top line. ①**Straight** to the baseline, ②pick up the pencil, start at the midline, ③**slash** down to halfway between the midline and the baseline, ④touch, ⑤**kick** down to the baseline.

/k/

Start at the top line. ①**Straight** to the baseline, ②**bump** up to the midline, ③**straight** to the baseline.

/h/

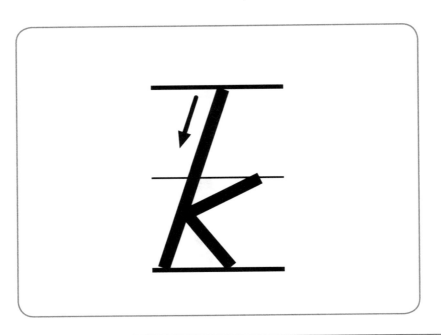

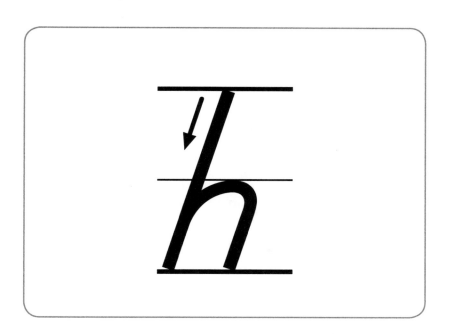

h

h

h

h

h

h

h

h

n   *Start at the midline.* ①**Straight** to the baseline, ②**bump** up to the midline, ③**straight** to the baseline.   /n/

m   *Start at the midline.* ①**Straight** to the baseline, ②**bump** up to the midline, ③**straight** to the baseline, ④**bump** up to the midline, ⑤**straight** to the baseline.   /m/

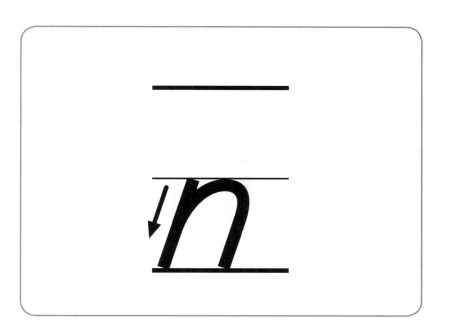

n

n

n

n

n

n

n

n

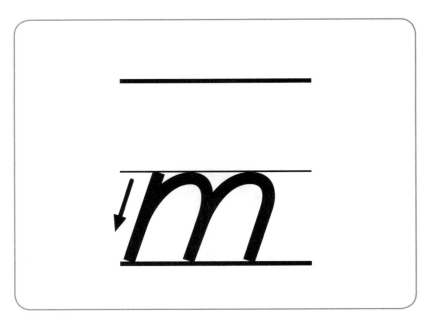

m

m

m

m

m

m

m

m

PRACTICE 1

i

t

r

l

b

p

k

h

n

m

PRACTICE 2

t

p

r

k

n

l

h

b

i

m

DROP-SWOOP LETTER

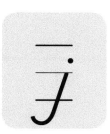

STROKE

DROP–SWOOP

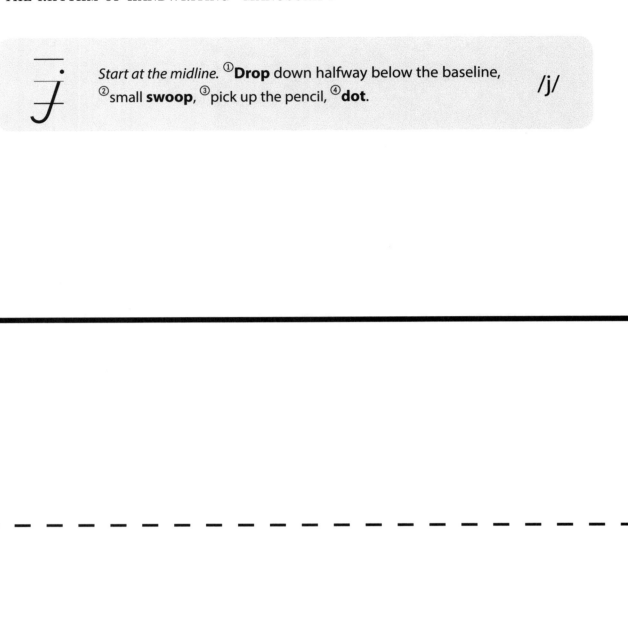

Start at the midline. ①**Drop** down halfway below the baseline, ②small **swoop**, ③pick up the pencil, ④**dot**.

/j/

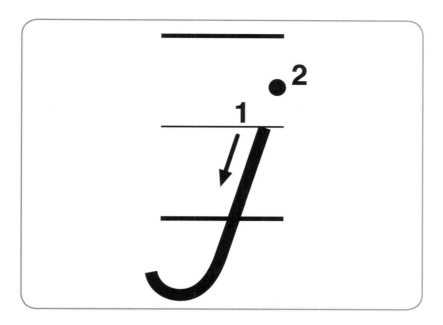

PRACTICE 3

j

i

t

r

l

b

p

k

h

n

m

PRACTICE 4

t

p

j

r

k

l

h

m

b

i

n

PRACTICE 5

j

l

i

t

n

m

k

p

r

b

h

Down Letters

$\overline{u}$ $\overline{w}$ $\overline{y}$

STROKES

DOWN

SWING	STRAIGHT	DROP-SWOOP

u *Start at the midline.* ①**Down** to the baseline, ②**swing** up to the midline, ③**straight** to the baseline. /ŭ-ū-ö-ü/

w *Start at the midline.* ①**Down** to the baseline, ②**swing** up to the midline, ③**down** to the baseline, ④**swing** up to the midline. /w/

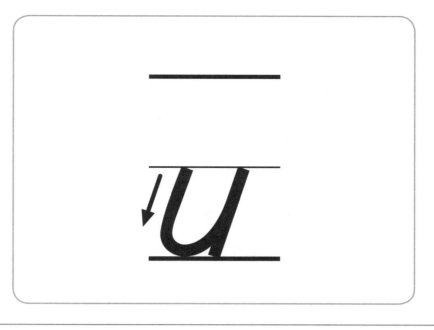

u

u

u

u

u

u

u

u

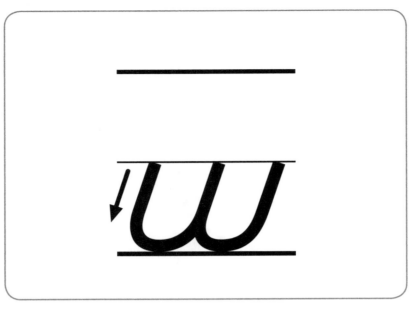

w

w

w

w

w

w

w

w

Start at the midline. ①**Down** to the baseline, ②**swing** up to the midline, ③**drop** down halfway below the baseline, ④small **swoop**. /y-ĭ-ī-ē/

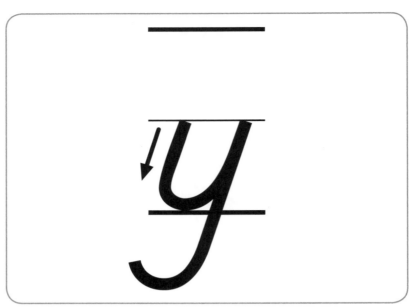

y

y

y

y

y

y

y

y

PRACTICE 6

u

w

y

j

i

t

r

l

b

p

k

h

PRACTICE 7

u

w

j

y

n

m

h

k

p

l

r

t

Writing Words

Letters within words should be written close together and evenly spaced. Between words leave a finger width of space. Read each word, then practice writing it. Use your pointer finger on the large words. Use a pencil to write the words on the following pages. Try to write each word with smooth, rhythmic motions.

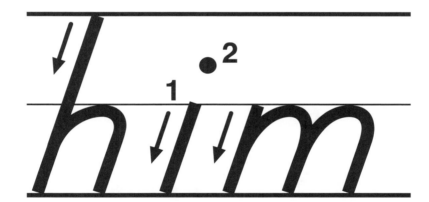

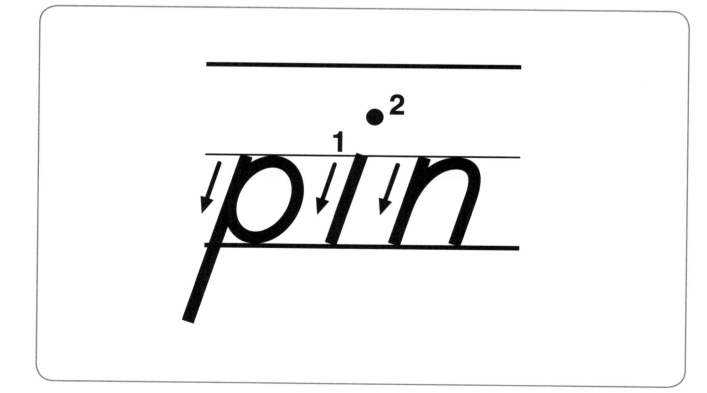

PRACTICE 8

run run

will will

tin tin

pin pin

hip hip

PRACTICE 9

bun bun

jib jib

yip yip

lip lip

kit kit

PRACTICE 10

jump up

hit rim

win it

bump him

trim it

PRACTICE 11

jump bump

in bunk

pump it

bill him

it will rip

Roll Letters

$\overline{a}$

$\overline{d}$

$\overline{g}$

$\overline{c}$

$\overline{o}$

$\overline{qu}$

$\overline{s}$

$\overline{f}$

STROKES

ROLL

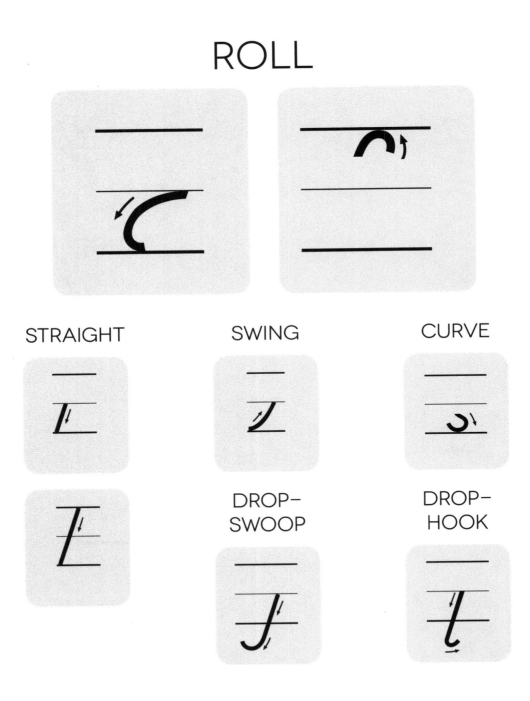

STRAIGHT   SWING   CURVE

DROP–
SWOOP

DROP–
HOOK

a

Start at the midline. ①**Roll** around to the baseline, ②**swing** up to the midline, ③**straight** to the baseline.

/ă-ā-ä/

d

Start at the midline. ①**Roll** around to the baseline, ②**swing tall** to the top line, ③**straight** to the baseline.

/d/

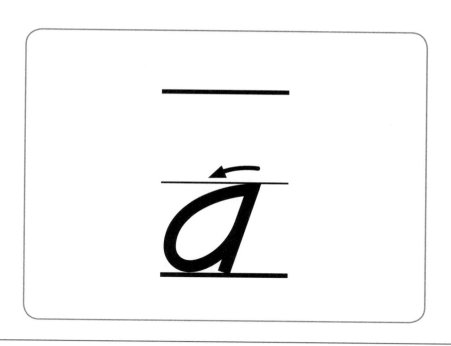

a

a

a

a

a

a

a

a

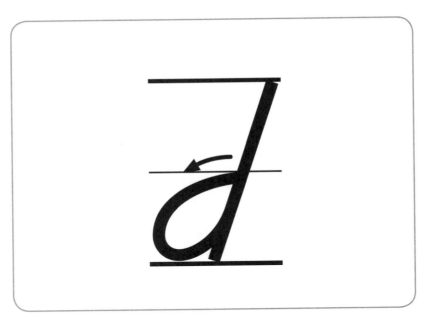

d

d

d

d

d

d

d

d

g

Start at the midline. ①**Roll** around to the baseline, ②**swing** up to the midline, ③**drop** down halfway below the baseline, ④small **swoop**.

/g-j/

c

Start just below the midline. ①**Roll** around to just above the baseline.

/k-s/

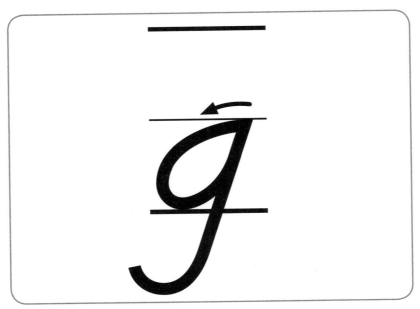

g

g

g

g

g

g

g

g

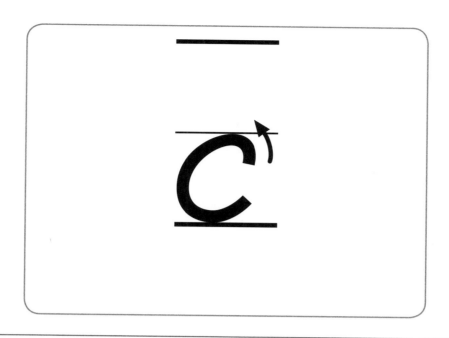

C

C

C

C

C

C

C

C

C

o   *Start just below the midline.* ①**Roll** around past the baseline, back up to the midline.   /ŏ-ō-ö/

qu   *Start at the midline.* ①**Roll** around to the baseline, ②**swing** up to the midline, ③**drop** down halfway below the baseline, ④small **hook**, ⑤pick up the pencil, start at the midline, ⑥**down** to the baseline, ⑦**swing** up to the midline, ⑧**straight** to the baseline.   /kw/

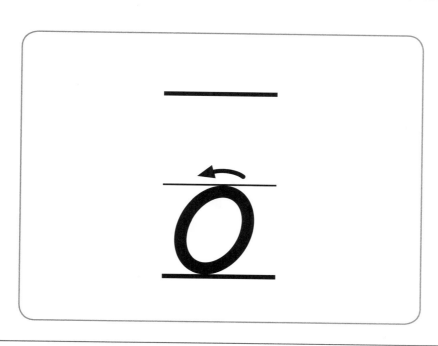

O
O
O
O
O
O
O
O

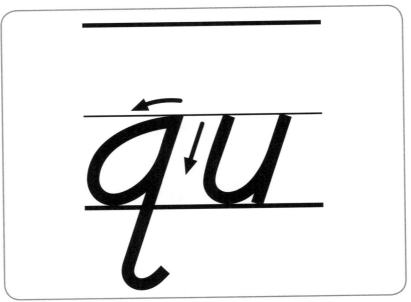

qu

qu

qu

qu

qu

qu

qu

qu

S — *Start just below the midline.* ①**Roll** around past the midline, ②**curve** back past the baseline. /s-z/

f — *Start just below the top line.* ①**Roll** around past the top line, ②**straight** to the baseline, ③pick up the pencil, ④**cross** at the midline. /f/

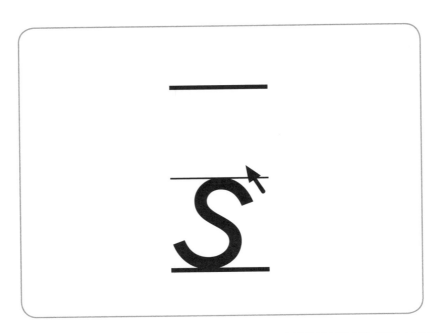

s

s

s

s

s

s

s

s

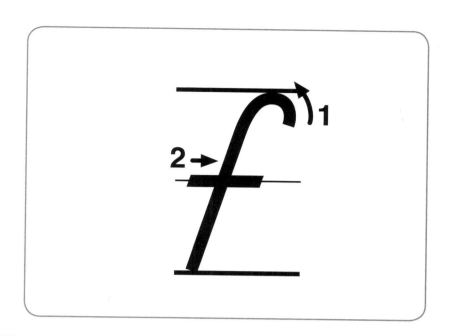

f

f

f

f

f

f

f

f

PRACTICE 12

a

d

g

c

o

qu

s

f

u

w

j

n

PRACTICE 13

d

s

g

qu

c

a

o

f

b

y

i

m

PRACTICE 14

y

d

g

qu

c

o

a

r

p

s

k

f

WRITING WORDS

Letters within words should be written close together and evenly spaced. Between words leave a finger width of space. Read each word, then practice writing it. Use your pointer finger on the large words. Use a pencil to write the words on the following pages. Try to write each word with smooth, rhythmic motions.

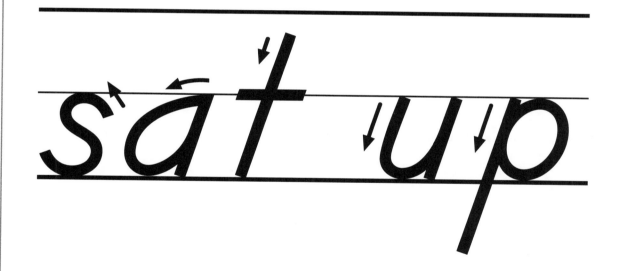

big dog

hug us

PRACTICE 15

pat pat

rug rug

sat sat

rat rat

yap yap

PRACTICE 16

cap cap

cut cut

quit quit

land land

pit pit

PRACTICE 17

it got lost

big map

fun hunt

dig it up

jump on it

sit on top

PRACTICE 18

big bug

jug drips

soft hat

hug us

dump sand

swim fast

SLANT LETTER

ē

STROKES

SLANT

ROLL

Start halfway between the midline and the baseline. ①**Slant** up to the midline, ②**roll** around to just above the baseline.   /ĕ-ē/

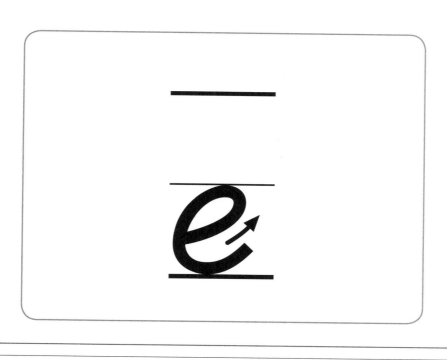

e

e

e

e

e

e

e

e

PRACTICE 19

e

f

s

qu

o

c

g

d

a

y

w

u

PRACTICE 20

e

n

w

m

t

d

h

l

f

s

qu

b

PRACTICE 21

hot sun

red mug

log jam

wet man

stand up

big plum

PRACTICE 22

men stand

send him

bent leg

sit still

jet lands

fun band

PRACTICE 23

his pet rat

it must win

it will quit

not yet

get set

yes it can

KICK LETTERS

$$\overline{X} \qquad \overline{V}$$

STROKES

KICK

ANGLE UP

SLASH

X   *Start at the midline.* ①**Kick** down to the baseline, ②pick up the pencil, start at the midline, ③**slash** down to the baseline.   /ks-z/

V   *Start at the midline.* ①**Kick** down to the baseline, ②**angle up** to the midline.   /v/

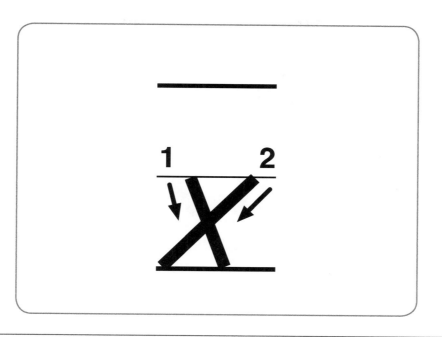

X
X
X
X
X
X
X
X

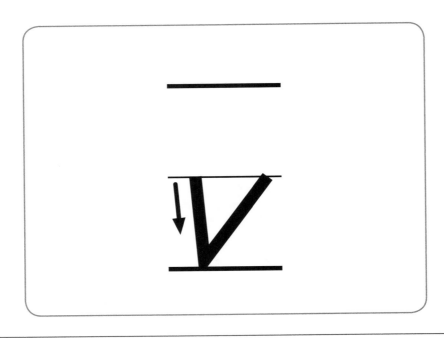

V

V

V

V

V

V

V

V

PRACTICE 24

x

v

s

m

o

h

g

d

i

y

w

t

PRACTICE 25

e

f

r

qu

v

c

l

x

a

k

b

u

PRACTICE 26

box box

beg beg

bag bag

bug bug

bog bog

big big

PRACTICE 27

fun stuff

flip flops

glad dad

pink vest

red fox

fat cat

CROSS LETTER

STROKES

CROSS

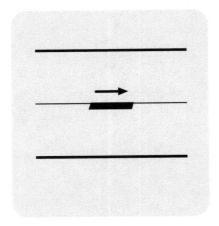

SLASH

CROSS

Z

Start at the midline. ①**Cross** at the midline, ②**slash** down to the baseline, ③**cross** at the baseline.

/z/

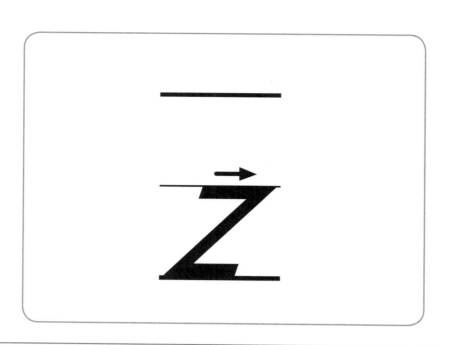

Z

Z

Z

Z

Z

Z

Z

Z

PRACTICE 28

x

v

z

e

f

s

qu

o

c

g

d

a

PRACTICE 29

pink box

it will run

zip it up

hot vent

six kids

in a mill

PRACTICE 30

fox trap

bugs buzz

soft fuzz

big cliff

bad bump

mend pants

PRACTICE 31

clip clop

slip slap

fist fast

miss mess

best rest

drip drop

PRACTICE 32

pet frog

cut logs

soft buzz

flat land

ink pens

flags flap

PRACTICE 33

pet fox

mint gum

red van

plum jam

pink crab

wet rag

Uppercase Letters

Straight Letters

I   I   H

P   B   R

N   M   K

L   E   E   D

STROKES

STRAIGHT

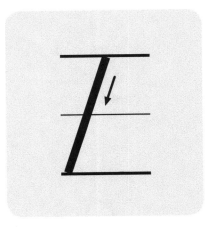

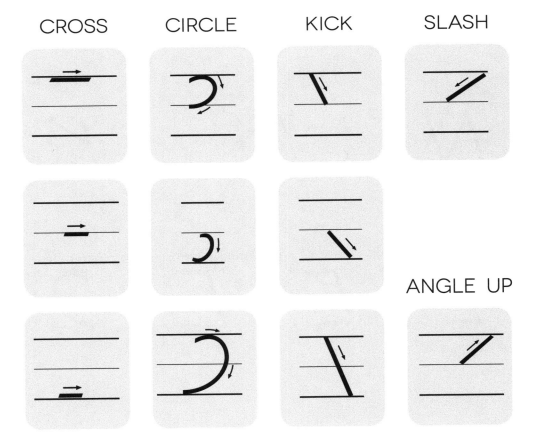

CROSS   CIRCLE   KICK   SLASH

ANGLE UP

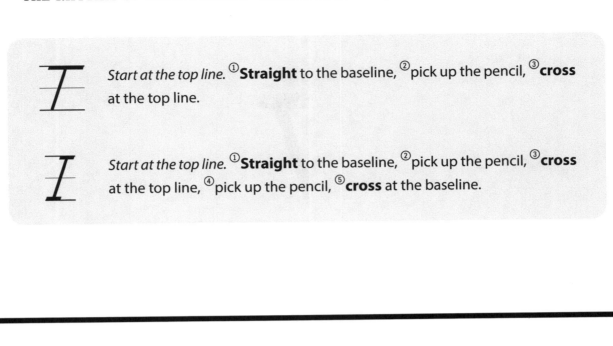

Start at the top line. ①**Straight** to the baseline, ②pick up the pencil, ③**cross** at the top line.

Start at the top line. ①**Straight** to the baseline, ②pick up the pencil, ③**cross** at the top line, ④pick up the pencil, ⑤**cross** at the baseline.

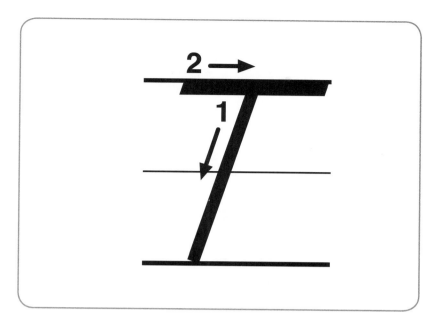

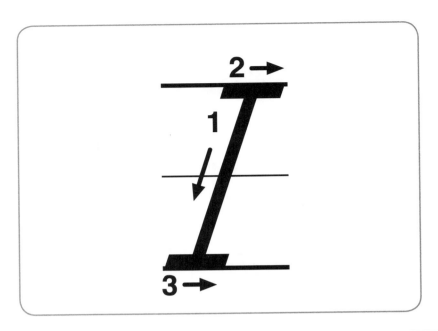

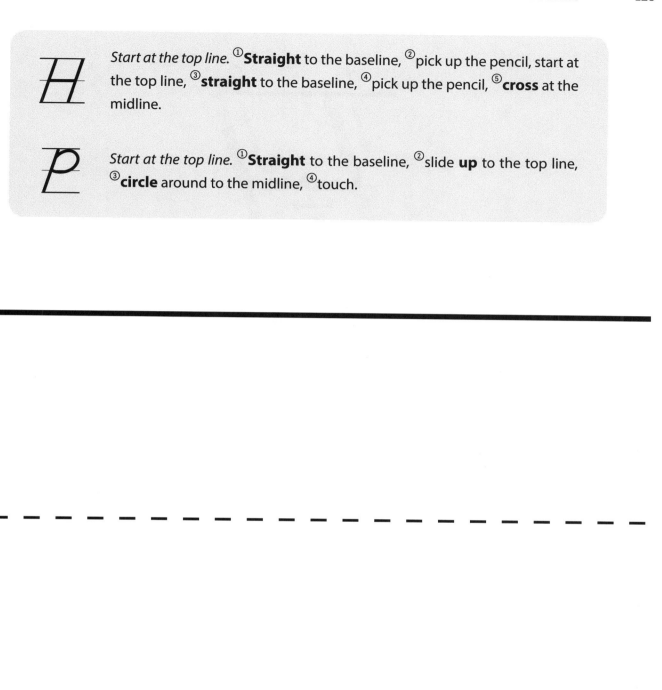

Start at the top line. ①**Straight** to the baseline, ②pick up the pencil, start at the top line, ③**straight** to the baseline, ④pick up the pencil, ⑤**cross** at the midline.

Start at the top line. ①**Straight** to the baseline, ②slide **up** to the top line, ③**circle** around to the midline, ④touch.

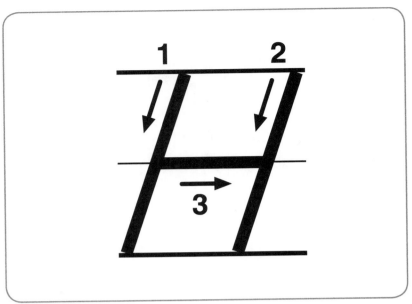

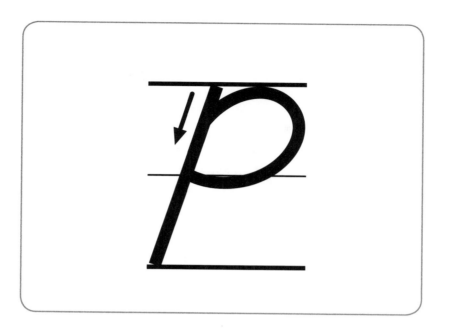

P

P

P

P

P

P

P

P

Start at the top line. ①**Straight** to the baseline, ②slide **up** to the top line, ③**circle** around to the midline, ④touch, ⑤**circle** around to the baseline, ⑥touch.

 Start at the top line. ①**Straight** to the baseline, ②slide **up** to the top line, ③**circle** around to the midline, ④touch, ⑤**kick** down to the baseline.

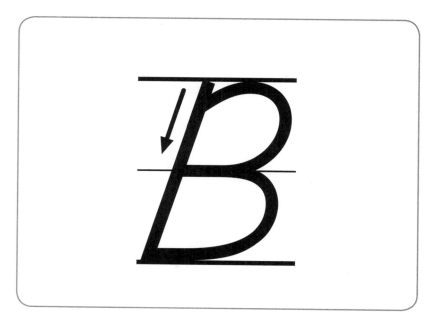

𝓑

𝓑

𝓑

𝓑

𝓑

𝓑

𝓑

𝓑

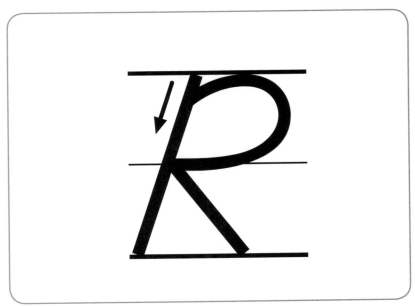

R

R

R

R

R

R

R

R

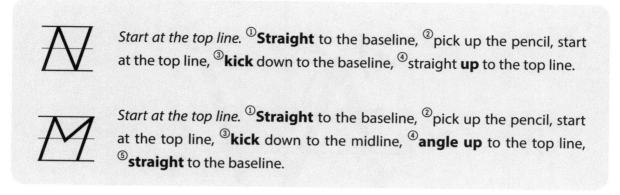

Start at the top line. ①**Straight** to the baseline, ②pick up the pencil, start at the top line, ③**kick** down to the baseline, ④straight **up** to the top line.

Start at the top line. ①**Straight** to the baseline, ②pick up the pencil, start at the top line, ③**kick** down to the midline, ④**angle up** to the top line, ⑤**straight** to the baseline.

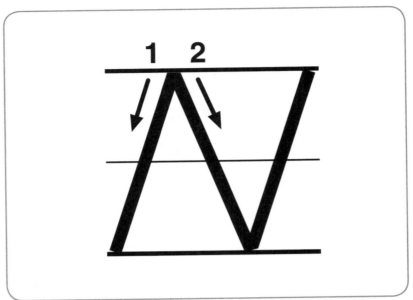

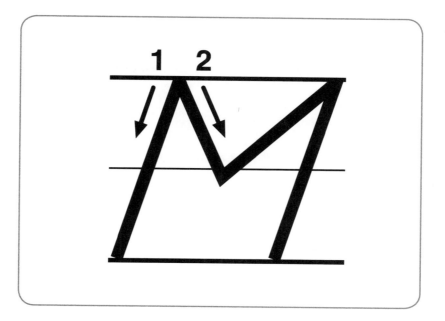

M

M

M

M

M

M

M

M

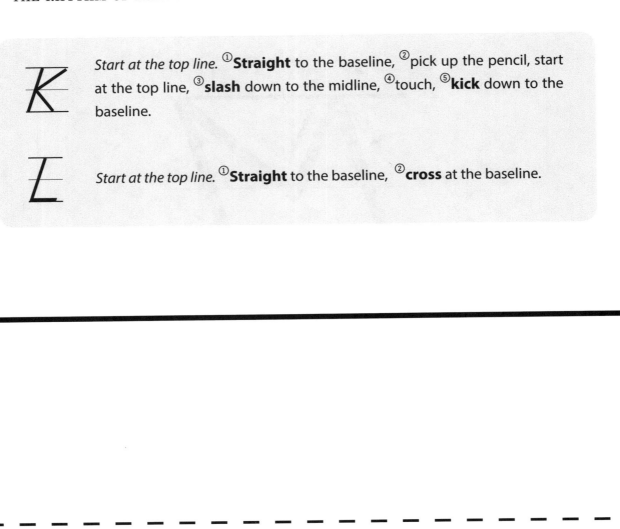

Start at the top line. ①**Straight** to the baseline, ②pick up the pencil, start at the top line, ③**slash** down to the midline, ④touch, ⑤**kick** down to the baseline.

Start at the top line. ①**Straight** to the baseline, ②**cross** at the baseline.

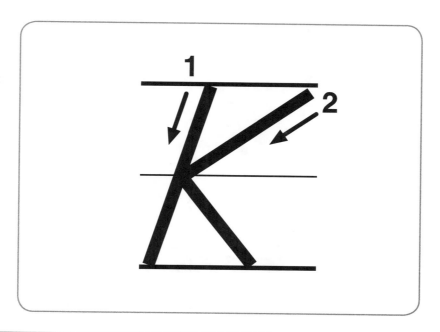

K

K

K

K

K

K

K

K

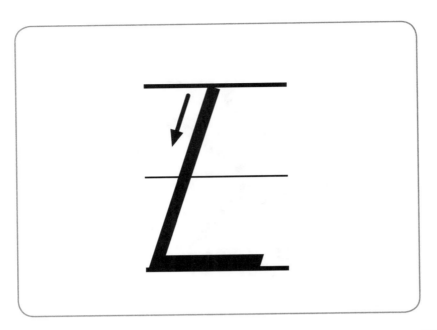

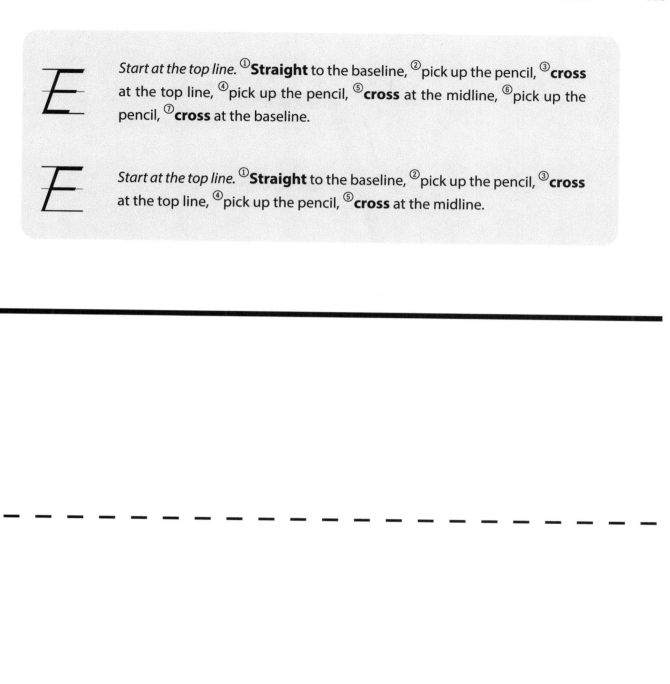

Start at the top line. ①**Straight** to the baseline, ②pick up the pencil, ③**cross** at the top line, ④pick up the pencil, ⑤**cross** at the midline, ⑥pick up the pencil, ⑦**cross** at the baseline.

Start at the top line. ①**Straight** to the baseline, ②pick up the pencil, ③**cross** at the top line, ④pick up the pencil, ⑤**cross** at the midline.

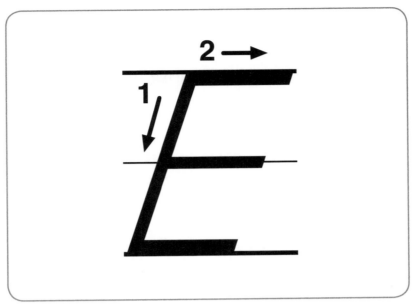

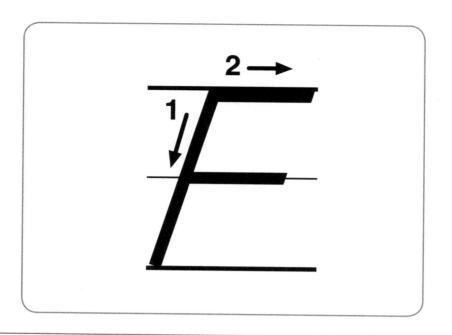

Start at the top line. ①**Straight** to the baseline, ②slide **up** to the top line, ③**circle** around to the baseline, ④touch.

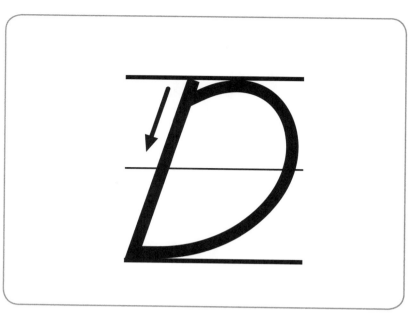

D

D

D

D

D

D

D

D

PRACTICE 34

T

I

H

P

B

R

N

M

K

L

E

F

D

PRACTICE 35

D

H

E

L

F

M

N

K

B

P

R

I

T

PRACTICE 36

Pat

Big

Rug

Nap

Mat

Kitten

PRACTICE 37

Hat

Land

Dad

Egg

Fun

Inn

PRACTICE 38

If

Bump

Top

Pigs

Bad

Run

PRACTICE 39

Next

Masts

Kit

Hands

List

Hint

PRACTICE 40

Dig

End

Flap

Ink

Rink

Tip

DROP-SWOOP LETTER

Sᴛʀᴏᴋᴇ

DROP–SWOOP

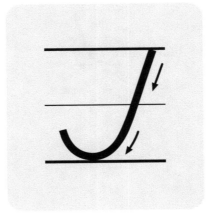

Start at the top line. ①**Drop** to the baseline, ②**swoop**.

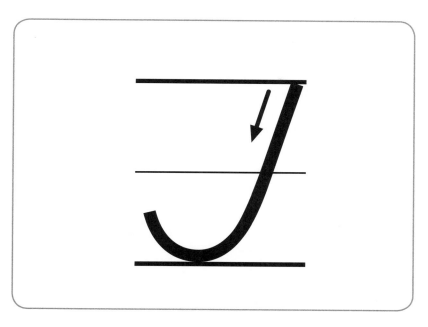

PRACTICE 41

J

M

E

P

B

L

N

H

K

I

R

F

DOWN LETTER

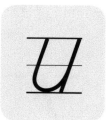

STROKES

DOWN

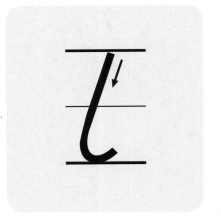

SWING

STRAIGHT

Start at the top line. ①**Down** to the baseline, ②**swing tall** to the top line, ③**straight** to the baseline.

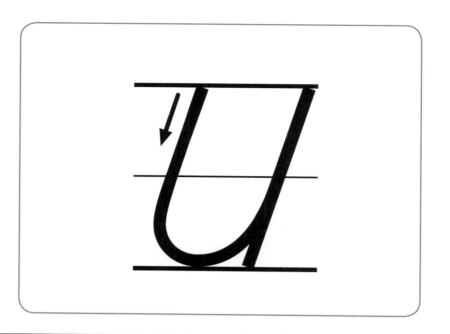

U

U

U

U

U

U

U

U

PRACTICE 42

J

U

T

D

E

F

N

M

K

R

B

I

PRACTICE 43

Job

Just

Up

Unless

Mast

Rid

PRACTICE 44

Jet

Twin

Illness

Plan

Band

Max

ROLL LETTERS

C G O

Q S

STROKES

ROLL

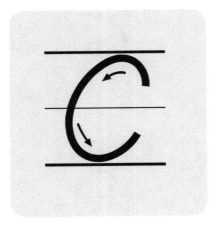

ROLL

DRAW

CURVE

KICK

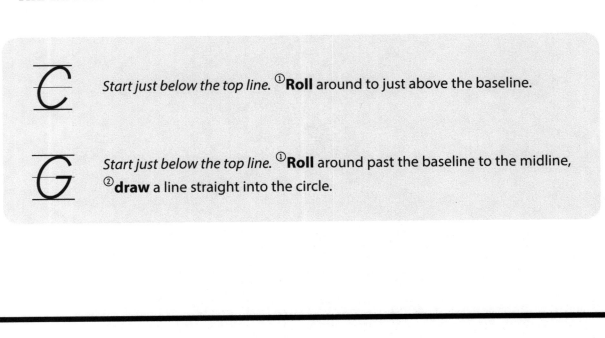

Start just below the top line. ①**Roll** around to just above the baseline.

Start just below the top line. ①**Roll** around past the baseline to the midline, ②**draw** a line straight into the circle.

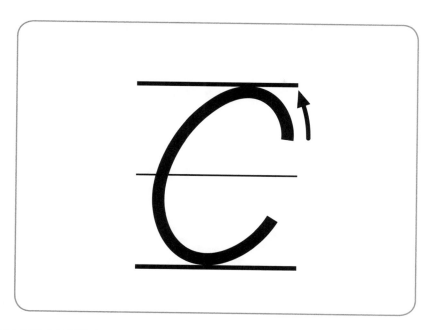

𝒞

𝒞

𝒞

𝒞

𝒞

𝒞

𝒞

𝒞

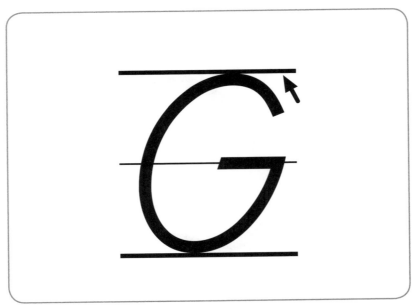

G

G

G

G

G

G

G

G

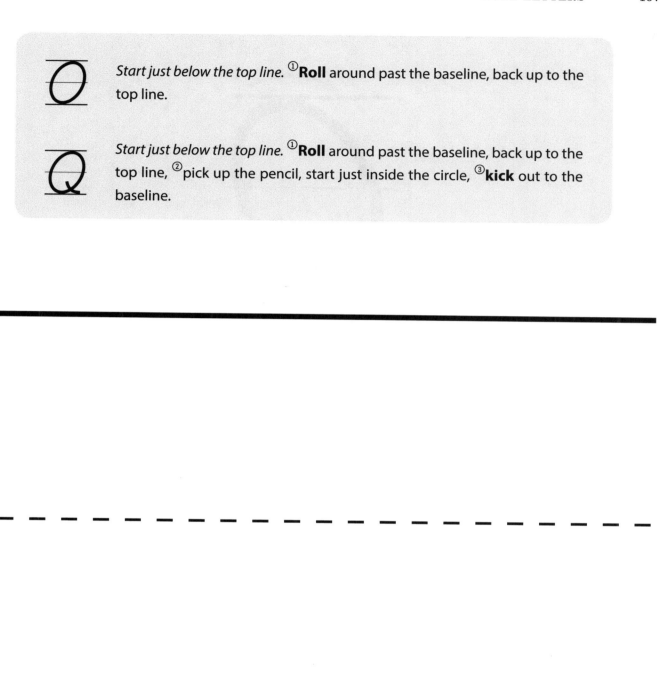

Start just below the top line. ①**Roll** around past the baseline, back up to the top line.

Start just below the top line. ①**Roll** around past the baseline, back up to the top line, ②pick up the pencil, start just inside the circle, ③**kick** out to the baseline.

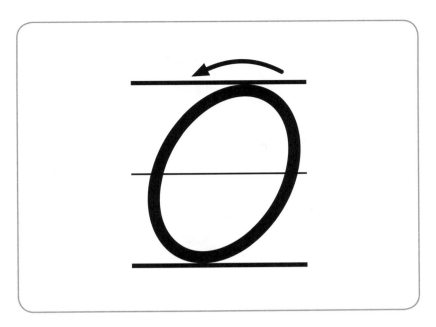

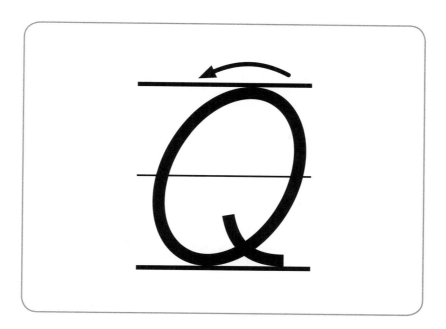

Q

Q

Q

Q

Q

Q

Q

Q

S *Start just below the top line.* ①**Roll** around to the midline, ②**curve** back past the baseline.

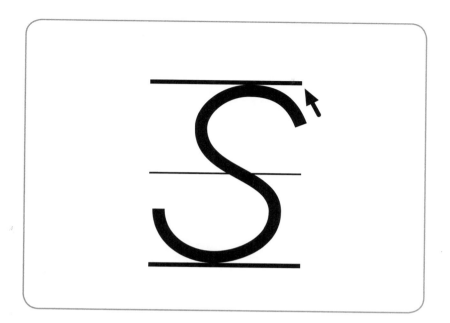

S

S

S

S

S

S

S

S

PRACTICE 45

C

G

O

Q

S

N

M

K

R

H

U

P

PRACTICE 46

C

B

G

T

O

I

Q

F

S

E

J

D

PRACTICE 47

Cats

Gap

Odd

Quit

Sons

Kids

PRACTICE 48

Can

Grin

Ox

Queen

Sam

Mud

PRACTICE 49

Net

Bend

Soft

Flit

Rust

Left

SLASH LETTER

STROKES

SLASH

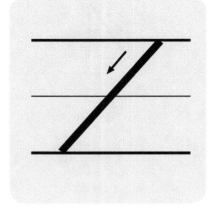

KICK

CROSS

Start at the top line. ①**Slash** down to the baseline, ②pick up the pencil, start at the top line, ③**kick** down to the baseline, ④pick up the pencil, ⑤**cross** at the midline.

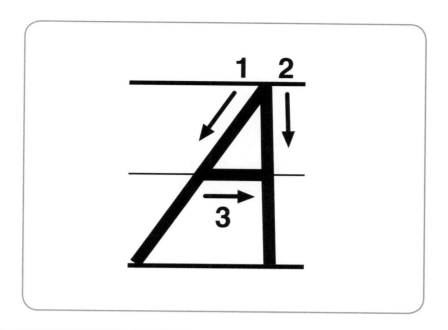

A

A

A

A

A

A

A

A

PRACTICE 50

A

J

I

Q

E

O

T

P

U

L

S

G

PRACTICE 51

And

Loft

Rub

Tell

Met

Drag

PRACTICE 52

Sat

Kiln

Blink

Get

Alan

Pan

KICK LETTERS

STROKES

KICK

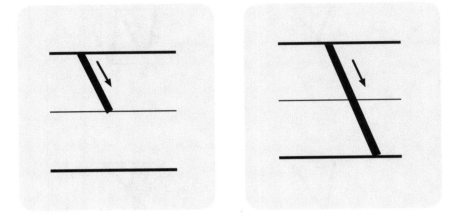

SLASH   ANGLE UP

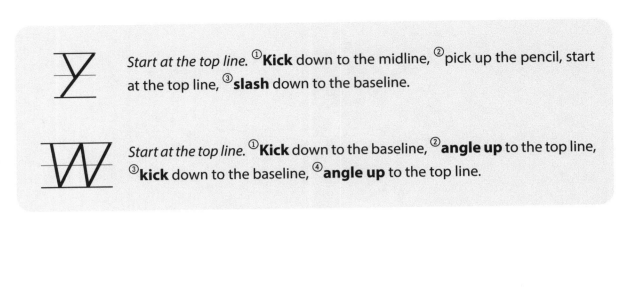

Start at the top line. ①**Kick** down to the midline, ②pick up the pencil, start at the top line, ③**slash** down to the baseline.

Start at the top line. ①**Kick** down to the baseline, ②**angle up** to the top line, ③**kick** down to the baseline, ④**angle up** to the top line.

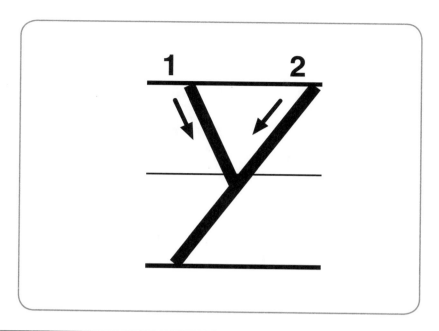

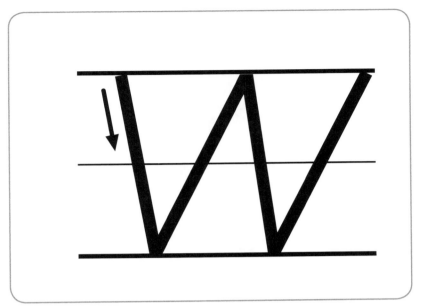

Start at the top line. ①**Kick** down to the baseline, ②**angle up** to the top line.

 Start at the top line. ①**Kick** down to the baseline, ②pick up the pencil, start at the top line, ③**slash** down to the baseline.

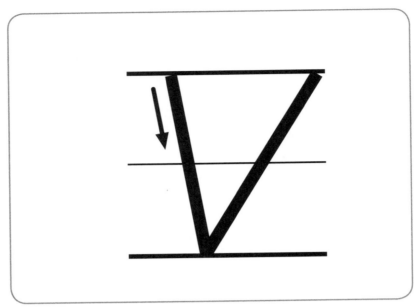

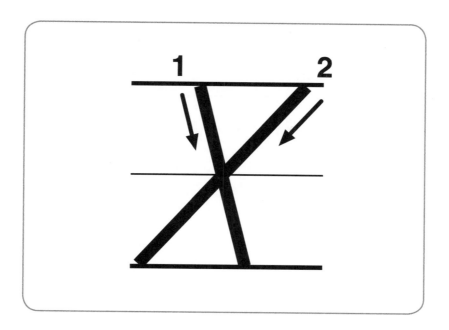

PRACTICE 53

Y

W

V

X

C

T

H

D

I

M

F

K

PRACTICE 54

Yell

Went

Brim

Vent

Craft

Hem

PRACTICE 55

Oxen

Jot

Until

Fit

Elm

Lift

CROSS LETTER

STROKES

CROSS

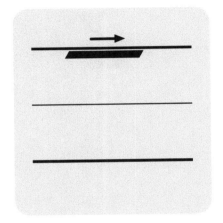

SLASH

CROSS

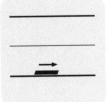

Z *Start at the top line.* ①**Cross** at the top line, ②**slash** down to the baseline, ③**cross** at the baseline.

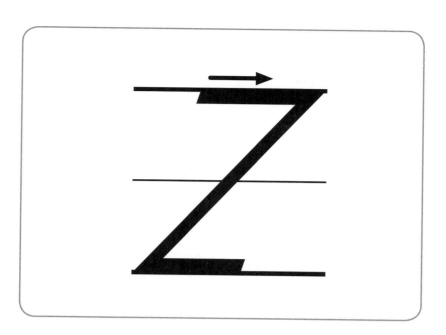

Z

Z

Z

Z

Z

Z

Z

Z

PRACTICE 56

A

Y

W

V

X

Z

S

B

D

F

G

R

PRACTICE 57

Ant

Yes

Will

Van

Zap

Mint

PRACTICE 58

Yet

Zip

Naps

Ask

Vet

West

PRACTICE 59

Act

Bat

Cup

Drop

Exit

Fill

Grips

Ham

I

Jug

Kennel

Lost

Milk

Nut

On

Plant

Quilt

Rent

Sad

Ten

Upon

Vest

Wet

X

Yes

Zip

PRACTICE 60

At

Bus

Crisp

Drums

Eggs

Flags

Glad

Help

In

Jog

Kit

Logs

Men

Not

Often

Pin

Quit

Rip

Send

Tents

Us

Vans

Well

X

Yaks

Zap

NUMBERS

1   2   3

4   5   6

7   8   9

0

STROKES

STRAIGHT

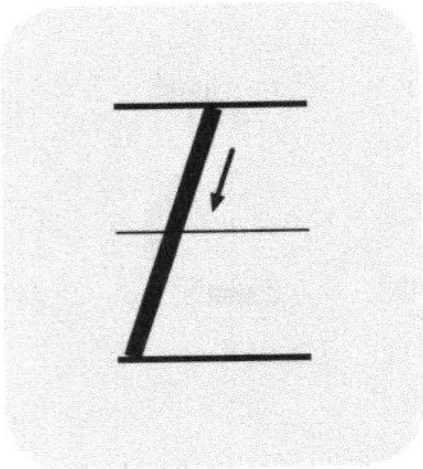

CROSS

ROLL

CIRCLE

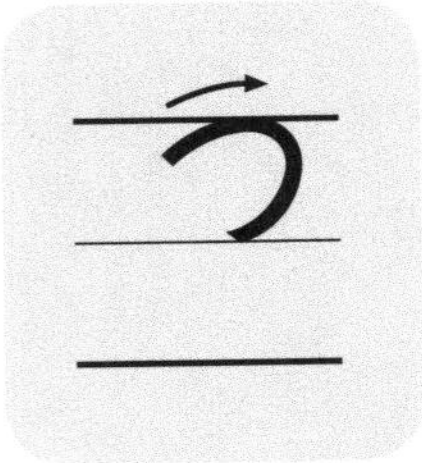

SLASH

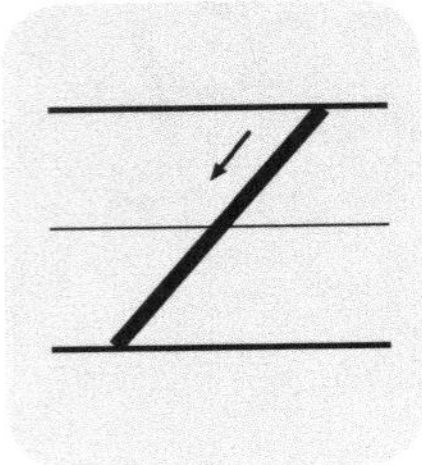

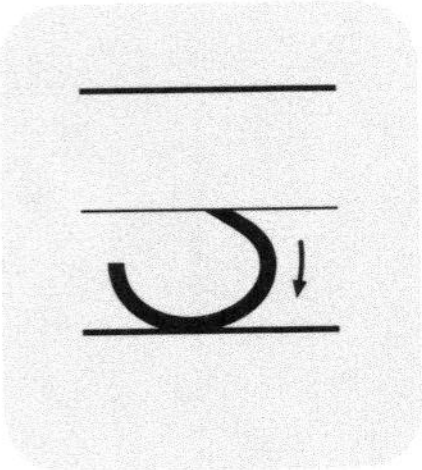

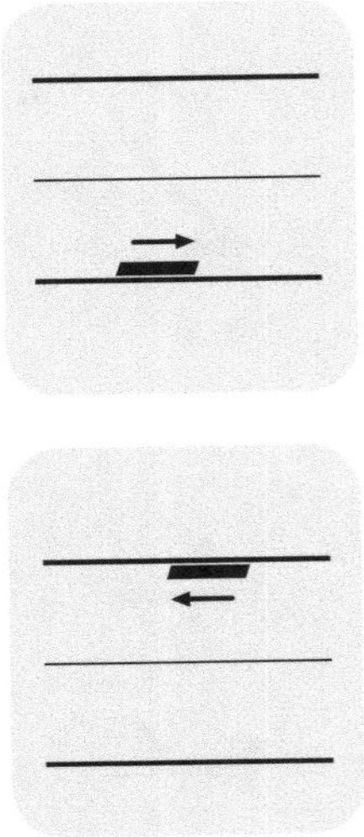

ANGLE UP

CURVE

SWING

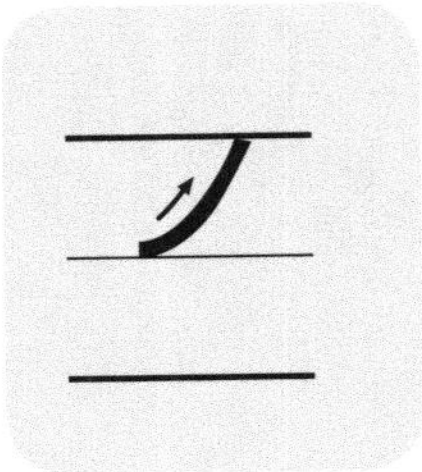

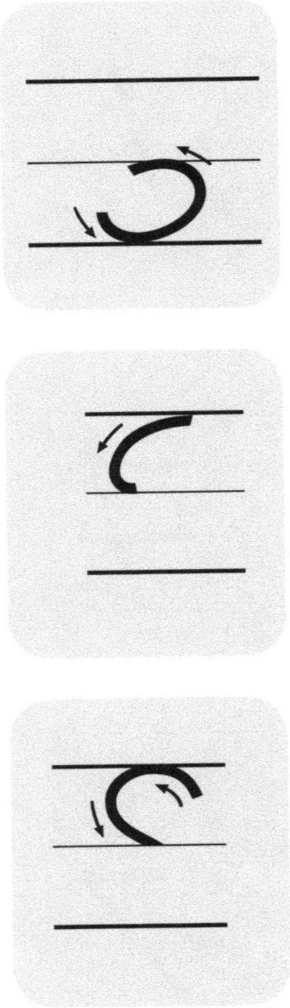

Start at the top line. ①**Straight** to the baseline.

Start halfway between the top line and the midline. ①**Circle** around to the midline, ②**slash** down to the baseline, ③**cross** at the baseline.

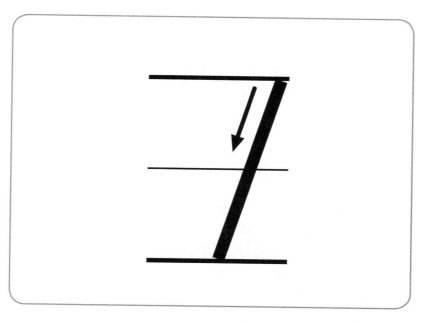

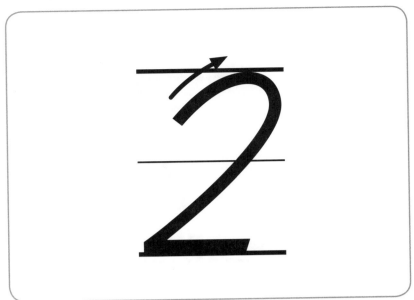

2

2

2

2

2

2

2

2

3   *Start just below the top line.* ①**Circle** around to the midline, ②**circle** around past the baseline.

4   *Start at the top line.* ①**Straight** to the midline, ②**cross** at the midline, ③pick up the pencil, start at the top line, ④**straight** to the baseline.

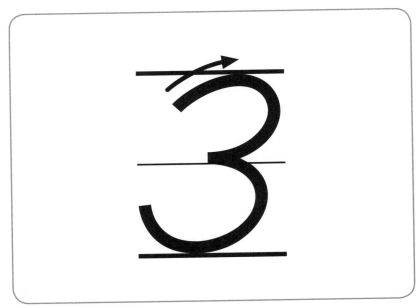

3

3

3

3

3

3

3

3

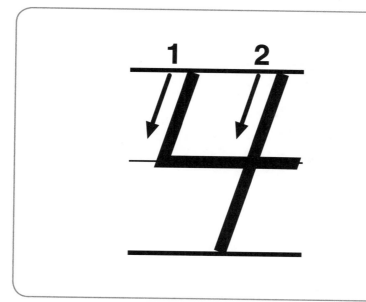

5 *Start at the top line.* [1]**Cross** to the left at the top line, [2]**straight** to the midline, [3]**circle** around past the baseline.

6 *Start at the top line.* [1]**Slash** down to halfway between the midline and the baseline, [2]**roll** around past the baseline, back up past the midline, [3]**touch**.

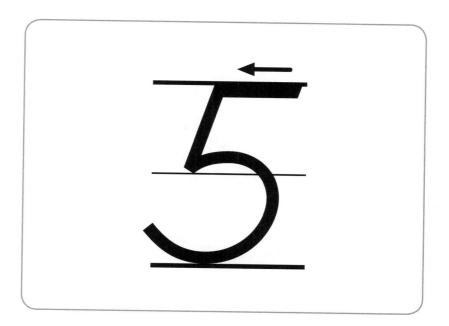

5
5
5
5
5
5
5
5

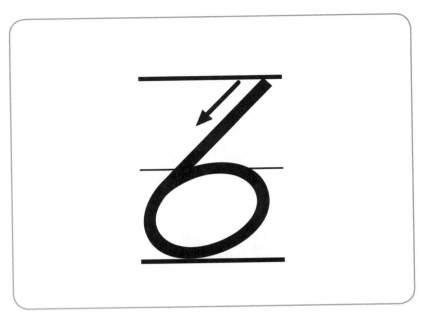

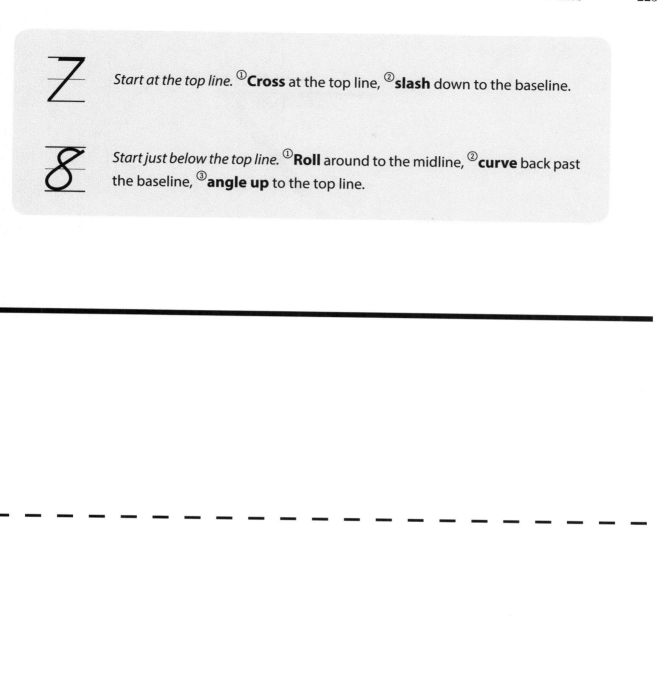

Z   *Start at the top line.* ①**Cross** at the top line, ②**slash** down to the baseline.

8   *Start just below the top line.* ①**Roll** around to the midline, ②**curve** back past the baseline, ③**angle up** to the top line.

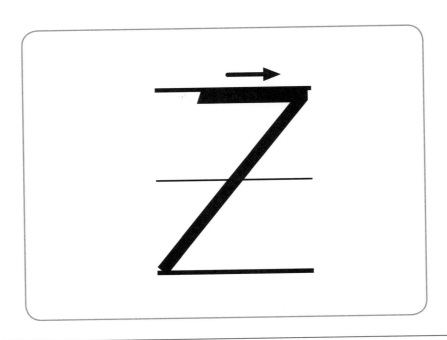

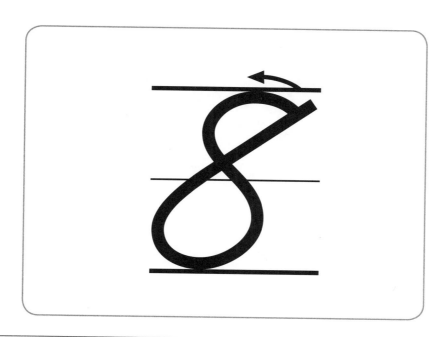

8

8

8

8

8

8

8

8

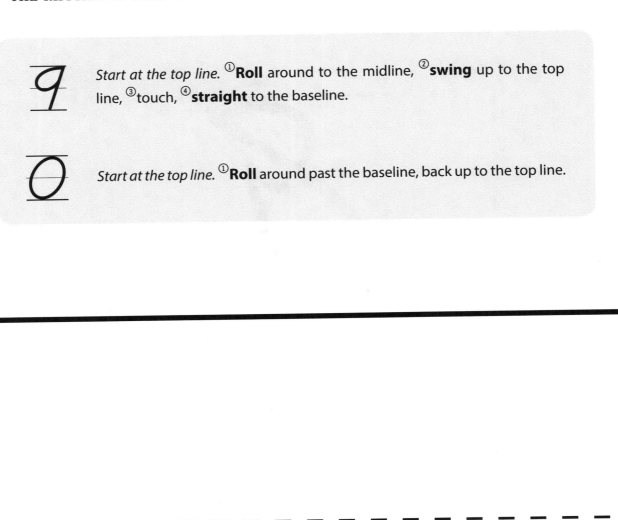

Start at the top line. ①**Roll** around to the midline, ②**swing** up to the top line, ③touch, ④**straight** to the baseline.

Start at the top line. ①**Roll** around past the baseline, back up to the top line.

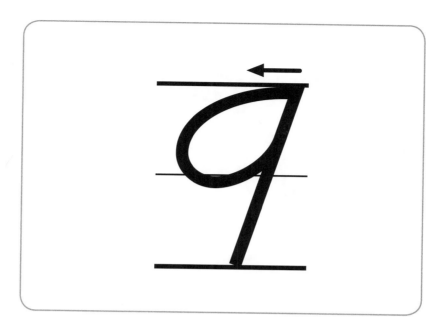

q

q

q

q

q

q

q

q

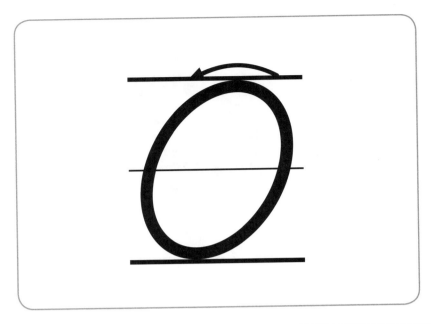

PRACTICE 61

0

1

2

3

4

5

6

7

8

9

10

PRACTICE 62

11

12

13

14

15

16

17

18

19

20

PRACTICE 63

0

zero

1

one

2

two

3

three

4

four

5

five

PRACTICE 64

6

six

7

seven

8

eight

9

nine

10

ten

11

eleven

PRACTICE 65

12

twelve

13

thirteen

14

fourteen

15

fifteen

16

sixteen

17

seventeen

PRACTICE 66

18

eighteen

19

nineteen

20

twenty

100

one hundred

1,000

one thousand

1,000,000

one million